D0621901

The Arcades

THE ARCADES

Michael Davidson

———————————

O Books · 1998

© Michael Davidson 1998
All rights reserved.

Some of these poems have appeared in the following publications, for which the author expresses thanks and appreciation to the editors: *Hambone, Poetics Journal, The Iowa Review, The Gertrude Stein Awards in Innovative American Poetry, 1993–1994, River City*.

ISBN: 1-882022-35-1

Cover photo and design by Leslie Scalapino.
Typography by Guy Bennett

Library of Congress: 98-068090

To my parents

Contents

I   SCREENS   11

II   THE ARCADES   31

     Foreclosure   33

     Agency   34

     Centrifugal   35

     Correspondence   37

     Dedication   38

     Disorder   39

     Drafts   40

     Emission   41

     Ethnography   42

     Exposition   43

     Gentrification   44

     Instruction   45

     Intention   46

     Leisure   47

     Mapping   48

     Pampers   49

     Parable   50

     Recombination   52

     Recuperation   54

     Resentment   55

     Restitution   56

     Solidarity   57

     Tapevoice   58

     Transcription   59

     Transition   60

     Transmission   61

     Zombies   62

     Translation   64

III CHRONIC   67
   The Analogy   69
   March 7th   70
   You Were Saying   71
   Footnote: Enthymeme   73
   In This Format   75
   Oct. 7   77
   The Autobiography Project   78
   After First Figure   82
   Rules Of Construction   84
   The Formula   85
   Polyp   87
   The Late Quartets   88
   Not Very   89
   The Quintet   91
   Blip   92
   The Canal   93

In a dream I saw barren terrain. It was the market-place at Weimar. Excavations were in progress. I, too, scraped about in the sand.

— WALTER BENJAMIN

SCREENS

1/27/91

These are moments,
I close the door, clank
in the collander
bottle cap, beans, potato peeler,
she wears a pink turtleneck
("I'm not your little girl; I'm Sophie!")
technicolor format of war
("Shell! Shell! Shell!")
reports of domestic violence
from the other room,
must phone P. in town a fortnight,
friend of friend
sequence of mumbled consonants,
could be report from the front
phone L. re: meet viz. Comm.
door opens, Saturday will take B A R T
whisk to hair, water falling in rotunda
(an illusion?) a designed rain
to soothe business
heels click in vaulted space.

1/28/91

Chords plus pauses,
air brakes in the distance
and the acacia is a little loud
a little early, bending away
from the fence, is it offended
by proximity?
one is not in the world
but in pauses (F. strikes a chord
then walks around) of the "Golf" war,
static can be sold along with the story,
correspondent is lost
and pursued; you hear clashes
as volume perimeter terminus alpha
in otherwise duration,
something marks time with flames
while something is the name of the present
like a bomb owned by both sides
and broadcasting from a bunker,
the city is and is not destroyed
unconfirmed corpses reported rotting
in the sun,
cloud cover high fifties no rain
bottlebrush stoical keeping time.

Blanched green washed blue
statice on the mend, earnest
purple pompoms, airwar stymied
by apparent collusion, generals stumped
schoolbus turns down Stevens
water truck airbrakes alert dogs,
Mr. Noggs grumbles near the fence
(dull thunk on porch),
landform awaits its yellow flags
defines catdoor or confrontation
with Norma over encroaching vines,
private colleges on endowments
defend Machiavelli
and the elder Pliny against film theory,
alert bird hops on fence, blast
of yellow almost knocks him over,
Islam is a desert with breaking news
line of soft grey scrub
declines east to supermarket
complex hidden from view.

1/30/91

Windows windows windows
schoolbus climbing the gradual hill
the phrase searches the phrase for what
discompletes it, start again;
incessant cough interrupts the dream,
we are having six in a public space
a seventh enters heaven to watch, I wake
the suburbs wake, break the final seal,
it says
our leaders roundly applaud our leaders,
the intention to seek something large
and yellow, phrases
are given latitude, planes take off,
Sophie sees a silver wing, says
it is her father,
9:00 sun arrives at fence, acacia bows
kindly towards the east, a feather
in the form of a pen bearing the name
of Pushkin, the building called
The House of a Thousand Windows
also called Narcissus.

1/3 1/9 1

The sentence places in a rhythm of things
things that replace others,
thus are we found and yellow,
without leaves
the plum reveals the fence, the fence
birds, the birds circle up
from the junior high, the bus (yellow) leaves,
Sophie, give me some words;
"Words."
Can you give me some more words?
"More words."
Like saying the universe
is made of light, names of the intervals
names of the particles in ascending waves
(hydrogen loves oxygen)
thus was a rhythm of numbers perfected
that began as space,
the general itemizes their losses
and projects a village as ours,
the press can read the sentence
they have left room for,
necessity of weaving
if it stops the burning of voices
for a moment, remains weaving
as in hair.

2/5/91

The narrator is compared to a shovel
he gives up his identity to become everyone
and smokes with Mr. Book the Havana at 25 cents,
we are parched but religious, we dream
when the sun has been drowned in smoke
we pray wherever there's room for a rug,
last night I was living by the train station
in the upper right hand corner,
I turn around and she has left,
gone back to the yellow building
and I follow through arcades
finding her avatars among solitary women
on public benches,
in others we are driving
through the lower right hand corner, maps
and their annual rainfall do not explain hands,
so long as we see the city in sleep
from a height of 30,000 feet
we are not yet awake
and thus not ourselves.

2/6/9 1

Last night I am downtown without a bathroom
and people in the streets
seek shelter in laundry boxes, coffee
is getting harder to find,
the greatest danger is becoming separate
and thus equal to the buildings
in which water has been drained
leaving only sleep in a doorway,
we wake level and exhausted; in these lines
I compare my love to my car, my skis
my electrical appliance, in another
I am prone in my dorm and crave yogurt,
trees confuse February with Spring
bursting in freshets of white,
we awake with a bad comparison:
the flour for cereal offering
the unleavened bread cooked in a pan
the offering mixed with oil
for which praise praise itself
has lost its voice in the desert.

2/9/91

This portends number,
glum laps in somber lanes
styrofoam takeout in the garbage
shaft of drill left in actress
and remembered next morning, national outrage
is expressed by members
waving tiny flags hats aloft,
war is on schedule, if deferred
by antiquities museum stuck
between antenna and bunker
cuneiform still unread in vaults,
that history will seem not to have begun
while we continue, Saturday light blue
white at the edges
but up close the fence wilts
acacia sends out feelers,
I think of distance, absent sun
under the spreading whatsit tree (must prune)
dogs think of breakfast,
I sustain moderate damage but emerge
with a shopping list, bottlebrush sending out
first red blast (jays squawk) more of same
to come.

Neal: "It remains a target-rich environment"
myoporum encroaches on acacia
yellow becoming progressively dustier
grey drone parameters rotate an axis
of calibrated defense, several gain access,
others wait in sun; sandstorms, religious holidays
and transmission intersect in manor house
from 9th century where they track the war,
Angles bearing gutteral consonants
meet flagellant Saxons in documents
plant rootcrops thence the Venerable Bede
and ecclesiastical law,
source of income for generations,
privet hedge rises above window ledge
while Murphy scratches around dryfood,
domestic landscape largely audible
largely foodstuffs: farina, dried legumes and fruit,
an occasional sentence in early spring
takes note of its predecessors
begins to sound normal
as a tree through a window gains
leaves loses bloom.

Out of the bunker slash shelter target
brown lumps of hair and matted clothing
on stretchers, redbrown red orange,
what distinguishes the body
without a word from other bodies
is a lolling of flesh, head hanging
over the edge
while all around, bodies tensed with purpose
lift, point, and dig; cut to Cheney
cut to Neal behind rostrum, cut to
commander in the field saying his
words; go lonely verse
to that capacious versus of thought
where blackened flesh of children hangs
like ghost laundry, surround gently what
these bytes have left behind, be balm
out of bomb, salve out of salvo,
tear out eucalyptus on the hill
that the earth beneath
might return in new forms, burn
the wood later but bodies burned in the name
of words return in forms impossible to say
and bereft of home, to these spaces
go and make miserable life listen.

2/15/91

Long night waiting at Emergency
for tiny bottle,
woke warm, cool grey
screen sky, one plane flies west
against it
George pulls up
starts weed whacker
gulls in spiral fan out
over the Triple A, are we vast
and serene as these columns claim
or portable, a box
made of cardboard
to hold letters,
Sophie's sore spreads
across her chin
I apply salve
but walls several meters thick
contained the blast
sent bodies flying through space,
the children could not be recognized
except for their size.

2/19/91

This sign could be unique
prevaricate in reporting these lesions or
predominate in the trench lessons,
repetition reduces strangeness to family
I recognize your image by your headphones
as if a network anchor secures a word
to the surface, these chunks of blue glass
with a view of the freeway
put in place by George
and stacked next to the house,
I like these sections of Winter
uttered at a distance,
she sees green by its difference from red
she pronounces the word most delicious,
last night we read the story of Max,
today we turn white,
if difference remains a shield, a sword
the image of someone in a suit waving off questions,
our reporter is the only person alive
and we are not alone.

Largely economic distress punctuates resolve
mutters among renters already smoked
and nervous, events fall out with scripts attached
citizens are alarmed or amorous, you could say
a dark man in a beret
causes a tree to fall in the desert
but by adjusting the mirrors
the forest will die of its own reflection,
small towns in the valley collect urban rumors
elect a short sleeved electrician
to the water board,
he kinda has a feeling about that sort of person
balloon lifts off
and a logo skirts mountains,
drought tolerant rock roses red blooms
pride of madera bombs bursting in air,
one argues with neighbor: a tree falls
from a weak root or the soil
in bench graded lots
but they won't listen; look upwards.

2/22/91

I prefer not to say we are killing other people
I prefer to say we are servicing a target,
(Bravo Battery Commander Nichols)
as in filling a tank or taking care of John
in the Men's, as in we're a service economy,
rustbelt factories sunk in red snow
lake glittering in the distance,
librarian in Dearborn boots up Babylon
(how may I help?)
investments kept sub-portfolio
available upon request
polite market offers incentives
controls pollution by making it expensive
you can buy a new car with a black duck
we are a nice, disturbed culture
many centuries old, honeycombed temples
to Sun, Moon and other attractions,
we are a soft target
for a male rhino urgent product straining
within central control; patience
plus language is a form of address
so small even money seems disinterested
and then we shoot.

2/24/91

One spot in door second arrested bucket
slight leap to high H
then folded into pin branch of yap
called myself: mirror jacked into phone machine
nothing more livid if seldom sprung so tight
flushed motions, essentially repellent
dialogues with the imminent father
in this farincacious sink
spring dazed declines the verb awaken
hillock lilac fuzzy blob (is it distance?)
thin, lacks vibrato, first strawberries
then corn, the permanent war, absent water
the shift from yellow to dead battery
point at door, fire, door yawns
scratching of rusty spade intransigent soil
sign reads save these crusts
from drive-in, jays pick twigs
quick after tree trim
renewed in olive blur a nest and high up.

2/25/91

Silver quilted truck serves coffee
by the almost completed firehouse
guys in hats sit on bumpers
dusty pickups down to the corner;
you can extend this two ways: outwards
from the construction site (story)
or downtown where real estate
checks the screen (system),
Boulez crash plonk, George
sights along white plastic pipe
lays in groove, inserts drip heads,
death averted through structure
Mrs. Winchester, heiress and table rapper,
adds rooms, cool eye
attaches tube to faucet, damp patches form
by the dusty miller, line of men
hands on head
stretch to the horizon (oil fire cloud),
if there is no earth to scorch
a fire by that name burns in the head
that "hive of subtlety,"
in whose construction
the West forgets its name
turns on the water
and waits for Spring.

2/28/91

The war ends and the rain begins
and begins to end,
jay's breast feathers ruffle
in a stiff wind, intermittant squalls
what's left is analysis,
troop flank deploy berm oil cost
of the small expended words, the long
guns kids ride in Kuwait City
postmarked Manchester, Le Havre, Kiev, Detroit, Osaka
our disinterested flowing water, settling in ruts
or sheeting streets.
wet screen through which a blurred garden
seems to flow, doorbell rings, someone
wants work, something
leaves with me that is not the cat,
we are responsible for pronouns abused
in our name, that there be markets abroad
to water lawns at home, that there be others
to take my place, Sophie wakes with horses
turning on windmills, someday she says
we'll ride 'em.

THE ARCADES

Foreclosure

An intention to whiteness
removal of the frame
removal of the sky and its border
where the flat of Kansas meets the flat
placed there, one is put
out of sight that a tilt sight
with distant silo, cloud flanked
and field
might remember position,
the placement sound,
and sense voice without angle equalling
a barn slumped into earth, hay spilled
in a blank field, the foreclosed
and tenantless grid
that an intention to whiteness
writes back, resists.

Agency

The eye is a product of history reproduced by education
— PIERRE BOURDIEU

Waking in thick system
replaced with a questionnaire
or implanted with readout:
apple = not salesclerk

analogy to Hyatt explains height
while product is dispensed on cards,
person is in the "up" mode
sings Gershwin unconscious toothpaste
person is colored square
heart among three pears, three n's

      the nul that was childhood
      the nul that buys first television
      the nul that serves breakfast
takes on the tray bearing posture of service

dream of Horowitz on tour
noodling over the Transcendentals
slice of the Berlin Wall
next to Nordstrom's

I forget having come or appointment
I blank on the linkup or do-over, simply
rectify choice as representative
and send bill

      as buy
      so bought.

Centrifugal

Everything promises completion
including the end of completion

I assume so many positions in a revolving surface
of fragmentary instructions to a hyperbolic
as if these assignments will by themselves
become the urgency of their senders, blood
fairly freezes while standing on a bus
among those becoming a ghost;

from this window
he gains a perspective on public
its branching directories of need and procedure
followed by lunch
an efficient machine that poses
for their greased necessity until the plane
tilts to reveal eating as a vector
produced by the speed of revolution that at first
seemed like Schubert, then became lost
in a halo of pastel sorbets

and spiralling outward
in dizzying traceries of hemoglobin
now splatters the facade of such edifice
that to erase names replaces performance in the breach
of medals; someone coughs
and we urge the manager to close the theater;

no one wrote the initial letter
thus no one can be blamed for its receipt
if you open an envelope
you are the subject of the sentence which begins
in the dream the mountains offered prospects
from the end of a road surrounded by acacia
in which nothing worked

I was there and am returning.

Correspondence

He conceived the plan of bringing two Persians to Paris where they would conduct amazement through their letters on occasional subjects. His subject is a book seemingly empty of opinions. On this point, we have constructed a fiction based on a city the size of a city. The distinction is telling. Plot is an enticement to elaboration, governed by a square on which stands a column dedicated to those fallen in its construction. The fashionable shops on its perimeter betray an Italian locution. We exchanged letters for handbags.

I woke quirky and vague among seagulls and silvery tuna. Limp bouillion pulsates in the dining car as I arrive at consciousness. Had I arrested sequence in the pursuit of a stable regime or would the display of handicrafts supplement a palpable boredom? The seraglio becomes a domestic version of the despotic state, just as this foetid car describes a religious intention. I hardly know where to begin and thus conclude.

I woke stiffly virtuous and relieved myself of anguish. A gelatenous archaism penetrates the Hotel Chopin at the end of a corridor of glass in which I am reflected among corsets and hosiery. Perhaps we have become these reticules trimmed in ermine, but I yearn for a pictographic writing. The age demands a stereoscope with candids of temples, pyramids and the spring beater. Implicitly our letters attack the state of frozen desserts while the cordial format invites penetration. Our empire is warmly regarded as necessary to their urban design. I await our experience with anticipation.

Dedication

This duet seeks some area not quoted
in the interest bearing public sector,
rain falls through it
praising the eyes of the unspeakable beloved
so that a house with its multiple
and walls merges segmented area
with your endurance, your many scarves
and the stoic machine
that prolongues eternity,
sitting alone in music we are sited
and gently swaying speak;

there have been sentences
ill formed in early morning but in shared
voices given heat achieve flesh
meeting as though Josquin were a square
of light and you the blurred receptacle
brought into optic and slightly
distracted by the black focus
of white noise emit sighs

these doors open onto a patio and sunlight
where a cat is intent
on something uncertain in the honeysuckle.

Disorder

Labelling my disorder helped make it more real.
— KAREN O'CONNER

These pointed fronds wave from a glazed cachepot
amber liquid beckons to become more
than I have dressed in the audacity of,
interest mounts; they need me
mirrors need me, the new fibers
imported crushed, tensile, a person
will arrest in the act
of secreting on her person through the ruse
of a mounded issue
unnecessary objects attached to an image,
helpless before marbelled and distracted planes
as "sick" becomes motto this cincture measures,
plants
in the libido until shoes address themselves
and the lapel adjusts to suit a margin,
I am as these models indicate wearable
nor has the volume
been kept low on purpose
just that in muttering a crowd will seem
to act without will and smiling.

Drafts

May not be letters at all
As fiery birds through a forest or indecipherable
On [Upon] the triumphant powers of Fraud
and Wrong, meanwhile I Endure
(on tempest-scorning eagles with cedars see...)

the hand tests a new quill
and at the base repeated profiles,
may be random letters or the trace
of something horizontal,
now a fire
from which sparks fleeing animals, thunderous sun
rising above freeway and the news
a businessman is stabbed in his groceries (Japan?)

erect and perfect and walking forth
but not passionless
waking and writing in the economy
while his postcard ("ordinary and/sublime relations")
returns commerce ("aureole and blue")
of a fundamental endurance

few pages reach fair copy
but remain mortal in the attempt.

Emission

Morning flecked with residual stills,
meat room at the corner apartment,
red door leads to the red door
then an entire scene returns
with a recognizable face,
Bob will perform for a price
the following and graduated acts
in the approved small
and perforated room,
we are watched and hydraulic,
tips erect and flushed with forgetting,
others could penetrate this temporary
and vulnerable square, their footsteps
remind us of contracts, forged documents
therefore we penetrate the sex cluster:

> room, city, terminal
> glass and steel lattice
> as if a garden of gyros
> had sprouted in civic green

roar of public busses on unscheduled routes
all the while smiling,
she, patient, he persistent,
they will not arrive
where destination carves its initials
in flesh, the state of emission continues
until we are only hands.

Ethnography

Wake in latticed light. Residual testimony left hanging like moss. Would pulsate but exit bland, stretch and make coffee. The body is a situation Mike is the actor of, sings aria "Come Bloodless Coup." Had been in C's apartment thinking of a word for money. Led to argument, veered off into spleen, and settled on Argentina, a sliver off the conversation. C proposed D. Then we had tea on the veranda. This was when I discovered tea in a novel by a big writer. Earlier, Pam had crossed herself with a conversion she had been having; husband Al described it like this. They grew to like their speaker, blending into a valley of chips.

If so, who calls on a carphone? The duet leaves only a head left singing after the dancing? Whose social is society? I come to Iowa with trepidation, balding at the truck stop. Invention of a speaker to do its buying having little language and a head for numbers. So many mothers want her baby, so many fathers describe breakfast as inadequate. One of these positions must be superior to all the rest if he is to get any sleep; the body wants time to think things over; by the river of Babylon, there I discovered photography.

Exposition

The silhouette of a person who escapes us. Seen from the side she is a repetition of *x*'s, the one to whom a letter is pointed. A classical figure facing the future as a point of defense or a port of departure, a four-gated city marked by railroads. In her hoops and bustles she is kept endlessly circulating, never sitting. Clothing becomes flowers. He intersects with metal, transient without progress. She wears a social order, hat upon broomstick, sabots thrown into machines. Thus the union was born of a series of nouns, poorly defined positions modified by exchange. She is turned into triangles, "walking bells"; she becomes a movable type.

At a certain point they discover boredom, an index of collective sleep. Mimed by machines that seem to whirr with a divine detachment one aspires to become a balloon. One floats above fountains worked by an invisible steam engine, fountain in the shape of dolphins, shells and aquatic plants.

We fall away from ourselves, drifting in and out of sleep, occasionally waking to wave a small flag. Upon waking we are already a moving crowd, able to be read. Observing the crowd from the standpoint of a Russian novel we gradually become a conveyance, a position, a plural. Something seen.

Gentrification

Seek remedies in the sleep margin
uncited men drinking and slouching
in transitional downtown, one
dances along a pediment on the second floor
another watches
to be in their threadbare
there must be electronic gadgets
in open air arcades, portable remedies
in the parking corridor
where the corner meets
another corner, accounts anticipate
these consumers in the big ledger
injections of an otherwise effluent
of a profitable share, the blimp
is a rentable vantage from which a pitched
ball becomes a Ford
while a struck glare and bombed basement
disappear from the front page
inconsequential as a mental recently released,
read these as an imperative attaches
to luxury and the intersections
will suggest themselves
much as a city creates signage
to give access to access.

Instruction

Lacked even good-bye status the miffed catcher signals yak yak we
have gales the permanent access to a blissed cottage and tours regu-
lar these splintered and constructed brackets yet retain yellow and
ochre tilted in direction of the assigned quadrants: one the back wall
two the foreground pink casually draped /C/ and the vegetables
that apply in order not to be spherical.

Supplemented once the seeds catch flesh and burn with unaccented
military backing while in the desert a famous breaks the crystal that
strikes an aging in his speech ducks and the longer necked birds
(burn is pleasure and costly) three of these flash on a literal horizon
producing copy.

Acceded to undress the pants bearing member one looks up from
doing and discovers a familiar these censored acts cost and repeated
metro breakdown soggy documentation soybeans sluggish for hours
lines advise where elements are efficient whoops or loop seem empty
without silos and steeples the family bankrupt pulls into a space it is
occupied water is an imperative also a substance.

Arrived at by the novel electronics a little circle consumes another
the backdrop rolls an extended Ohio or Underworld the principle is
obstacle field hand eye complexity and the result end dividends kids
eat small /O/ that when purple and extinct speaks recognizable
letters experienced as foodstuffs.

Intention

Ruling out intention
tennis shoe option nailed in Korea
and sold without fanfare in Compton
it's raining light bulbs
active wear third floor
these franchise in the salmon zones
flanking boulevards, purple medians
of agapanthus, frail and stooped.

Statistically viable on pension
negotiate walk sign by the tire store
and supplement with sheer product
pavement and turn signals blazing at noon,
transient, loose and signless,
peering through glass at a cordless phone
cans of flat latex in pyramid
remains cool, hat reads logo.

Until an excessive intention donates a sign
Large Free Drink Fries Riot
turns offramp into enterprise, the Chamber
lights a smokestack and hugs table.

Leisure

The impecunious or marginal of an otherwise leisure
consume labels at eight percent,
blunt instrument of sequence,
imitates the fantastic of trauma
until these dead animals arise in opera
and wear their wearers;

everything points to it,
the tip arranging a posthumous quick
and then descending for absolute
as coitus will leave one plumb if damp,
you had been inclined, coerced, bludgeoned
to speak of a casual purchase,
what is an intention
when the weather grows warm?

Among rows of eggplants and beans
an arranged Summer of widely separate
and sluggish, the leisure
of change, friends humming Handel,
drift through the Family Section
like conspirators hanging from meathooks,
the system offers itself a raise
and grateful takes it.

Mapping

In one way all shoppers may be cruising grammarians.
— MEAGHAN MORRIS

Back of the wake lay something black
peopled with familiars clothed in such
or actions stuffed with portent: point
and a person shuffles, buy
and a stranger smiles,
in this arranged and portioned glass
one finds the known, the vestige
of a lived that can be carried
in a marked sack to the next
western village with ice rink
hill town with subterranean pool
parking with vegetables; a woman
pushing a pram is snapped
from an eye in the roof, image developed
in a humming room she is not permitted to see
but in strolling, not buying
extends, complicates these aisles
until meanders seem pointed
where upon waking for a brief
moment one is lost

save your receipt.

Pampers

Following the verdict
clothing seems to fall from racks
under starched neon,
a boot in the window
brings a phone to the corner
to hear glass, shouting of hightops
in a glow at the edges
that creep closer to a toaster
or vista of infinite diapers
in Concordia near inevitable yogurt;

nothing is impervious to wear
when a collective mannequin
buys better hair,
yellows shade to browns
until we are last year's plaid,
pastels have returned
and the logo given a fresh coat,
these enterprise forget waste
when defined as product,
in the all night sale
we can recover everything

I am lost in aisles.

Parable

These books are essential
on the blank of us among ads
and the effect of a novel
on white consumption,

often writing merges:
jane and james share suds
on a verso
is written their ardor

ego loves ego, arcadian chair
addresses gazebo
in a sequence of washed frieze,
the retreat from Pompeii

the advance on Herculaneum
as a history of ash
with excessive explosion
among emerging banks

as dunes become ribs
in a shrinking blank
lit by an installed
and foreshadowed sun,

"her people
are patronized by ranchos
and manana," a metaphor
on the recto

describes something these books say
are tomorrow and useful
like the train of reason
leaving the station of class

from the farm of agency
I was once the happy subject of
and bearing sun looked up
could not read this

and wrote
these furrows

Recombination

I think I reticulate
among the harsh sentences,

an alphabet of subjects breeds
in a formerly white and hyperbolic,

speaking of the rubber check,
porous pocket and other political
our chair declares null
the liberal pail, water
is 50% possible
in a possible chair,

we squeak following the airbrush,
Don pumps for interpretation
scattering the seemingly permanent
and stocking the mildly plural
against vestigial by noon,

turning back into cyburbia
I write Dick for an offprint
on "the unknown Iacocca,"
fortunes of the mildly exasperated
inspire trust
while resting in the plausible primitive,

in that form of alienation
bells announce quarters,
we wake continually in a revived
if antisceptic rural

not sleeping in the recombinant city
is like sleeping anywhere else.

Recuperation

Once accumulation led to writing and writing to the voice marked tape. Thence miracles of removal until I am a problem to myself, the one in the little blue hat. Pigeons flutter about a statue of firemen raising a hose, the fog perpetually at the top of hills.

Although we receive these feelings in reflection soon we evaporate and are left with a convenience store. Not heavily, but it was 1969, we were a mass of denial. First it seemed we could see beyond the state and then that their buildings could be occupied after business hours. Beyond the marble grid, rhetoric perfected itself through our organs of pleasure. Emotions recollected in television where in solidarity with images we charged the Pentagon and, in its own way, won.

Resentment

First reign in Arcadia, second starched in panopticon. The gross seer packs a sack with spatulas, slotted spoons while the lesser temporizes on metropole. Requisite shepherds hard by hayrick and ruined weir, water still at the brim films over at edge, descends. Beneath pane swim glazed trout, ceramic angler casts thread in several arcs attracting flies. In this dream they are fearful of crowds, prefer doorways and the love hotel, small cubicles of progress save parcels lovers covet.

Fashioned into cunning time, space seems to improve: first the swain in buskins then the agent with yellow dray, then the writer of epistles in couplet. The scheme braces for apotheosis as the streets lose their dust. Sewers improve with each successive reign. Science leavens at the science fair. In the other dream he is waiting for you in a crowd, discerns a yellow dress; she smiles and the crowd parts like someone familiar. From a distance the masses resemble copper poppies waving at a priest. Disruptions of the display, purple and headless mannequins in the Spring line. He stoops to peer at Spenser in the window, glass stares back in alluring nods and becks. The word's fair ornament whom this bower sells at two pounds eight's a shelter maze and sky.

Restitution

Now he is sleeping therefore I am reading.
Geography is defined as the currency becomes stable.
I recognize my silence by the length of your sentences.
I become lighter by believing in science.
Part of my conversation lives in your aversion.
Part of aversion is confirmed by my needing to speak.
I have been invented by science.

Had I confronted him there in the reading room
He would have been disarming with chagrin,
I remain a window, eye of transparent malice.
He stirs in his sleep, and I turn into a greater spider.
Buy this flush valve and meet plumbing codes.
With helmets melting they fought the fire.
The health of those who relied on the building
Was in no way impaired by the loss of their files.
You are necessary to the message.
This was a challenge to the message.
Others ignore you based on the inflections
You recognize on the tape.
If I read these signs as necessary
I become necessary and pursue volumes of white light.
He stirs in his sleep because this is being written.

Solidarity

Things being pulled by men
men shaving their heads
in support (cut to shoot
cut to skeet, arcing, blasted
brief shot of sky)
in the drive-by
neon flashes,
someone salutes, a girl declines
into a national story,
I border on excessive waiting
I place words on a condition
and we become thick,
the directives of golf demand stories
beginning with *d*
       deregulated
       disunion
       diminished
       dancing with Gene Kelly
ethnic barriers erased in beer
all of the *t* words convene in Trenton
where the rivers cannot spell Whitman;

with man you have fatigue
with tv you return to Greece
where the word begins
and the expert does the numbers.

Tapevoice

Here in the tentative machine first forays
into self as stretched skin
port negative seeks rudder first woman swims channel
second summer boots password I buy wherever
link terminals with alpha blunt warning
open files or die (flags wave
air bogs in the midwest, kisses baby)
certain commands are parallel like weep
and rain, season has a fuck option,
messages return with intention to embrace
we are optimistic as we escape security
strategic use of humidity guns nervous
another goes unmentioned, "I" am in index
substitute imperative "purchase new files"
wait ten weeks pay supplement
achieve green life, "Bob" refers to card
which placed releases barrier, horns honk
screen darkens with impressions while truck
beeps backing this free commercial
and generous coastal scrub now grid
is subjective,
voice repeats Cheerios, Oh
I pronounce these vowels as my own.

Transcription

Had been dreaming in the arcades. Attempted to dial but fingers were thumbs, eyes blunted to numbers. The odd neighbor writes again. Finds us out after twenty years with his unusual hand. Crawl spaces revisited in an epiphany of penmanship. Went down to the mall in a vestigial intention, ordered the Arlington Storage Building. Flipped through fliers for insulation and protective screen. Parent was livid. Tried to convince, but Time is a Ford.

No one prepared us for the loneliness of children. A cry in the dark some hulking shape out of Goya. Old wedges of night, screen door banging behind the restaurant, marble top, galley table, brick and board. In a page, reading and sleeping all day. Maybe catch some waves in the morning. They say interesting things like actually and dinosaur.

Toxic floodplane with a smile, the old restitution of hands, work as a measure of pleasure. One wakes to hear sunset confused with rainbow. "She" becomes "her" as the agent of possession. Her doesn't want these clothings with sleeves. These emporia represent us looking in. We learn to possess our bodies, language, The God of fire, the God of substitutions. A man gesturing in his Ford is selling a boat to no one present. Someone wakes in suburbia and needs something.

Transition

The brown silence of an overstuffed apartment
slightly moist below the garden
in which we find the iris lamp
and the glass hand,

yet we love to make ourselves complex,
to twist and straighten, torment language
as though a body were a piano and the soul
a panorama of whirring wheels,

these tormented dreams of infinite city
with their conveyances forged
in a Hell decorated with grapes
are erased through psychology
and a three minute egg, toast
lightly browned,

the Gallery of Machines
flanked by plants, banks of orchids
where turbines conceive
a second Eden,

what I have lost in conversation
I send forth
in glass and steel
fantastic lens of the present.

Transmission (for Robert Duncan)

A forest or a field. Am I in the reading or is it reading me? Light
through the fence, vapor lifting. Into the clearing for a better look.
A lake that turned into a meadow. First field, first fealty. Then I
learned how to read errency, tracing the lips moving before the
sound forms. Which eye sees me and which the wall behind, which
bear is a weir bear? The unutterable cadence as a wave or train
swept up in these intentions of light. A soul living through speech.
Then came the age of the tape recorder. No word is crossed out,
everything lives and is holy. Seeing across Lake of the Woods I was
more than myself; I was called sight. Exasperation with the
luggage, with the tickets in the multiple pockets, with the electri-
cal connection and the instructions more than himself speaking.
Metal iris casts multiple yellows on a round table. In its halo an
occasion for speaking, the cut glass vase the pewter creamer
among the company. Present and speaking.

Zombies

Moving on to policy
blue lights at the boulevard palpitate
through blank air
prodding a sleeper
into restless jeremiad,
shoppers in shirtsleeves
guys with yellow stakes
furnish civic with a warehouse
first logo then buy shares;

I was in malls
friends were buying wallets and guns
as normal music pumped
through the narcissus corridor,
teens were contagious by telephones,
what is improved is the passive
while tax makes silent, soothing speech,
those had been ghosts,
now with earrings
and biceps of money become text;

waking in a jungle
the owner ponders agency
was I dream or campstove, are these
hollows infinite with mortage
and fifteen years, the shapes clamoring for flesh

are actually money seeking heat
they spy you emerging from accessories
like a fresh wind
and follow you to the elevator.

Translation

Against the black sea of a black night
a single light
of the duty free shop, blazing
on a broadcast horizon;
all the drowned sailors
are restored by its siren;

Deseret changes; old neighborhoods
are an allegory one steps through,
the predictable and repeated windows
filled with the glass of novelty
that by wearing becomes new
as a pilgrim arrives refreshed in Jerusalem;

I think of you, hapless shopper
stepping through mirrors with a map of Troy
only to find yourself
frozen in representation like a swan
in Audobon, dead sweaters
roam the aisles searching for lost husbands;

Within the cloacal streets of the old city
that gather like phlegm in the throat
new boulevards form in the mind
of a white architect nearing the end
of a life spent
among the dark consonants, the mass;

We would be signs
dragging once snowy plumage
through ravaged construction sites
that progress raise visible portions of itself
to explain the benefits of speed
the violet frisson of acceleration;

Where was Africa?
someone in an office of tusks
on the fourteenth floor asks
and in the absence of palms and musk
a museum of masks retains these black
distances behind protective glass;

In the aisles of exile
I think of forgotten sailors
who search the horizon for a solid thing
when wings are signs of harbor
frozen like script in azure
and bring back junk for the stalls.

CHRONIC

The Analogy

There are movements in the Sun
of which we are becoming aware
as the surface of the pond
shivers at my approach, gold
and grey shadows dig
into deathlessness, a big word
that means not extra, not politics,
they understand that an explosion
on a distant planet
is really a lake on the world,
a blue lozenge
into which we dive from a high rock,
later it serves to explain
the language we need to say
please put your hand
into this paper bag.

March 7th

In the letters I appear as substances. They find the correspondence and infer something beyond his words that applies to them. This letter never refers to you, Dear M.

In ten years one performs the mouth, but muscles have since atrophied, skin slack upon the jaws. The audience experiences silence being eroded over time.

Brief history of redness softly repeated.

I had inferred from your postcard that the world was read. One showed an avenue of plane tress stretching through a park. Another showed an empty shopper in an arcade framed in light. I inferred from your digressions that the word was red.

At this time the dream of becoming naked in a public space became possible. Refuse was swept into convenient drains and a piano was invented on which to play symbolic logic. The triumph of capital reflected in clotted passages beneath plane trees.

My poetry is genetically inclined. Reference to trees, swamps and voiced alveolars must be rejected along with strong coffee and shouting. The voice emerges in the late nineteenth-century, following photography as a tinny quatrain that once was afflatus. The genes did this to me and the words followed.

You Were Saying

almost immediately
I will approach boredom
not the same
as a thinking stone

falls in the ear
unlike
the phone anybody
might verify

J.
she lives by the canal
where at one
the ships glide past

under the word for mis
fortune
everything is erased
or null

until what is said
is regarded as such
in the factory
in the lecture

where I am not reading
but filtering water
as an anemone is said
to breathe

now
all of the diversions
have become
single, in the pool

one hears with the bones
a body dissolving
floats as if torn
by saying her name

or her name is broken
in boredom
the bridges raise
and the ships sail

as the city sleeps
we begin again at 5
nothing emerges from the mist
yet we see light

to swim to convince
I feel sleepy
in the conference
in the reading

until glass forms
against transparency
a ringing in the ear
not an eruption

an interruption
of evidence
that to recommence
hardly notices

we will meet
by the bridge
having used these words
not as a crowd

but an interested party
the phone is felt
as its words
so we say

of the poem
but the sound
of water sloshing in an ear
in which a crowd

appears
at the place become familiar
and often
but several persons

in the square
a column casts its shadow
on those who died
in its honor

Footnote: Enthymeme

If it be great praise
to please evil men
but necessary
in which the new

becomes a film
of novelty
performed there
a missing term

proves we are living
a man with a home
decrees the unfortunate
leaving dung

this is one example
a stable home
is not a premiss
for one in the wide world

something cannot be discovered
even though we had looked
every day for a week
on our way to the lake

and picking up
opened a door
that has learned
the lake

to please good men
is unfortunate
given a square
of which the novel

thing is not proportion
but the action
performed there
that proves its opposite

even if homeless
we become bored
as horses
in a private yard

of which privacy is the nature
and a door
opens into squalor
alone or in numbers

a key in the grass
gleams
when not looking
we saw something unexpected

what had been lost
familiar to a hand
expects what comes to be
parallel to the lock

a mirror in the morning
and the reflection disturbed
in our diving through
is not mine

that in itself owns nothing
agency
is not freedom
to say anything

In This Format

You watch the movie version
thunder rolling over suburbia
until the faint splats hit the skylight
and you're awake, framed and gone

in a variant you reserve a space
on the word "word" for a better
less muted blank
(the heat they made stunned goers)

you can't do that, Hank avers,
and his students support him,
rain has been falling in Antigone
where everything conspires against class,

to make a constant white phone
accept the caller from the Côte
d'Ivoire, Hi
it's the same middle c

you can't duplicate
by importing sets from St. Louis,
a bed stage center
is still a bed, Desdemona

forestalls the pillow with a willow
as a wife becomes a knife
with a bone handle, the crowd queues
at dawn to watch,

this is hardly language
although they mistake a phrase
without antecedent
for the supertitle, Lucia

for a brief moment goes crazy
in English, they say
we need rain in hot weather
they say we need fire

and then she phones 9 1 1
he's banging on the back door
"you have his record"
she repeats

before being cut
off
I walk with a blind man
away from town.

Oct. 7

Across these intervals
with grey and flat buildings
intervals of green
their bushed borders
where if they are blown down
the structure could be read
as flat
on someone's table
you wouldn't choose
to come here
yet they do
their yellow hats
and red lunchpails,
one chases a truck
for the ride out
to the parking lot
the distinguishing thing
is the trees
that hide the design
it says here.

The Autobiography Project

I is a desk
I could also be writing my life
Their Desire is My Concession

flash block punt concussion adolescence

then came the erasers
a lyric meant something
men wore hats

I couldn't write this
without a voice
I contracted into a foetus
and blew myself
back to the neocene,

there were vessels
crossing the page
the pain of the rowers
was compared
to the pain of a new nation,

the nation is a desk
with some beads and masks for support

blip germ plasma genetics perception

give this man some water
and the question of perception was
(this is the good part)
am I getting closer to you

bombs bursting, the Trilateral Commission
COINTELPRO (verdant pampa)
area studies, the invention of philology
and is "is" the subject
or just an excuse to repeat functions
I secrete I confess,

the man wearing a pumpkin
had written his memoirs,
we were all writing ours
reading each others' for the dates

I pressed her into print
behind The Crowbar, She forced
me into a taxi in front of Plumb Bob

I keep returning to this scene
in whatsits name
in which whatshername meets the guy
that played the lead in...

I forget
the cells reel toward Roussilon
a blasted tree
resembles a blasted tree

he had been cleared of his earlier crimes
and was warmly welcomed into Argentina

there was a colony of lepers
among whom he lived unnoticed
gradually losing his past
until all that was left…

I repeat am not the votary
of words as such
nor of surfaces
though others have so concluded

the public has been erased

that Summer we explored the docks
in shorts, television
was on TV he was just a placeholder
"endlessly signifying"

like as morph so glyph or look

because to look is to act
or the other way around
then came the Marshall Plan
and the walnut console

body hair and secretions
were in the distance
I was never raped in the gym

but Indo China was already
on the map, see these islands
and you think of water
see these targets…

he emerged from the bunker
a quote from the Vedas already
in place, God

makes me do bad things

After First Figure

Wolf marries the Princess
but first he undergoes wandering
and questions it would take a lifetime
of cold

to answer, to understand water
sink to your knees
at 60 below, to understand blood
become a carrier

of the gene marked x,
I was imposing in green
I was exposed in Arcadia
where the forest is a condition

for repeated commands,
find me a stick
and I will draw a magic circle,
burn the stick

and you can buy another
down at the stick store,
what was in a circle rises
like a colloquy among barbers

they converge and exchange rituals,
food is catered
leaving time for knocking on trees,
trading amulets, the etymology of testimony

in testicle, this book
is these books, I have grown
under them like moss on a fern floor
yet they point

at the Bay, the bridges
on a windy day
you were there, a little
to the left where the freeway

no longer continues
asking about the sign
and there was Robert
not looking and talking.

Rules of Construction

In the present
will be understood past and future
in man
will be understood woman
in the third
the first turns into a stone
the second has escaped into vapor
and the sequence will include the sequence.

A camera placed at the entrance
will show that a worker
can be seen coming as going
if he enters
at the time of the explosion
his body is an exception
which you can see in Exhibit E.

When the machines hum under the lagoon
the desert will seem to grow
of its own volition
the volunteers will merge with orchids
until a system under glass
will exchange carbon in a vacuum
with the other stuff
Dante proves this
with his image of…

The Formula

was a dream,
it was not a dream
but like real life,
I was in a dream

called The Projectionist,
I am before them
without notes,
they are to listen

without ears,
I am in a tree made of ears,
the clouds are below or above,
the birds are also

flying or forming an alpha,
it was like real life
in a real sentence,
we are late in violet rain

made of rooms extended, in one
he finds his childhood home
the crawlspace of conjecture,
in another a mother shrieks

with laughter,
the formula includes the statement
I am in a dream
and the persons who occupy the center

in which the preterite dictates
a past I could have lived,
he was in a city filled with stones
he was a quotation in a city

filled with books,
searching through the stacks
he discovers Zion and Alpha
Centauri, once there was a man

who exposed everything, he was
more than one, once
a man was so discreet
that people walked through him

on their way into other bodies,
invisibility is a sentence
unrolled in a glassed-in car he repeats
while driving through rain,

the formula depends on closure
which he achieves by thinking hard
of what to say next,
then the curtain opens

and Buster dives
through a pedlar's tray
and disappears through her body,
if you think the end

you awake as stars,
as shadows
of distant light.

Polyp

This Summer they are replacing the voice
with consonants performed by lips and tongue

that penetrate your mouth when we speak
and find ourselves in what sound furthers

then the anemone opens, flutters and folds around
the sound of water, the letter five

I can't pronounce these silences without damaging
us, the little phonemes we practice

before replacing the receiver
what else is the voice for if not the social

bodied like blips on a grid
so that if an island is invaded by sound

language is waiting to speak it into hats
and medals; I read the paper silently

not believing anything, but "we" seems to be speaking
in its vowels, the u into which everything pours,

the A, foreign to myself, on a good day
I remember the infractions as clearly as a ship

on a good day something has been written
and speaks back.

The Late Quartets

Things diminish in the late quartets
absence of blue against blue tile
body shrivels in its exercise gear
until violins are violence in the register
purchase vacuum discrete ledger backyard
of the voluble syllables, poured
in the good ear, in the other
enigma spraypaints lozenges wearing muffs
a formula documents distance she drives
portions collapse miracles in votive
while dozens erect spires,
one feels these lacunae as yellow breeze
pushed by leaves, residue of Summer
that corrupts the skin until a lemon
you wheel out umbrellas for a late lunch
some fit of plurals misses the overhanging
leaves that as canoe touch a diminished shore
you were once attached to oar
and witness act as water ear
could be lake could be late.

Not Very

In that we were moving and had been moving for some time although nothing had prepared us for the arrival of the package which brought back Providence, city of graveyards, our first visit to "The Evergreens" closed for the Winter, the Shaker settlement at Stockbridge and a claw footed bathtub in Boston surrounded by travel books you are responsible only for those portions to which you gave assent while the rest is their business let them deal with the repercussions the rain was heavy then less heavy until the Mad Scene when it poured.

You know which avenue of escape by the emphasis given to the third category, the one that brings him to his knees and then you drive off listening to the flood which has drawn the sympathy of our leaders, gas stations under water some of his anger emerged in a letter the system protects by permitting equal access, in a perfect system something is left over which drains into the cavities supporting the brain.

The perfect union he envisaged was not yet complete but rapidly being annexed in the west what was missing was a song whose theme was the perfect union, the men who inhabited its outposts, their games of chance, their dogs with reference to climate and indigenous populations in an idiom they could understand on which he was putting the final touches when they broke into his house and destroyed the press.

As it were objects appear more than expected from their description in the catalogue but the cost had not accomodated our need for them during a week when the system exacted more than the usual expenditure and the memory of these events did not prevent rain or prepare a chicken with garlic but achieves an integrity in the present similar to the dream in which she returns to occupy that sofa purchased last year with coupons saved from something, she was still angry we were still awkward they were too understanding in their support.

The Quintet

We who live in the silence of the sign
now think in the opening bars
of the c Major Quintet
of a silence its deepened bass
displaces, summer in blond grass
fallen plums, apricots
softened in afternoon heat, that chord
increasing in volume
crossing the green porch and over
the orchard, has displaced
with its dark changes,
the boy one was in sound
returns at last
in the anticipation of what falls
after the last bars, what sound
does the head make in remembering
what youth retains
beyond these heard forms
borne on air?

Blip

I'm on the summary side of the mesmer, stalking this sheet like an allegory from Tustin. Let down your furr and they flip you, levitate and you're from Boston. This kind of schedule is bolgia. You recognize an old teacher, and the smock jockies have her in carcinoma. So they build up a portable and bomb the principle. Wish I'd had that sleeve to put a schedule into, but they gave me the three-day job someone left for the adjuncts. I might as well rob a turkey as serve their skeleton; they might as well hire a temp as pay me to sweep up their rinds. If you're unemployed you can be a kid. Over in recomb they retrofit a new worker, complete body suit from an out of work actor. That's me all over: the mural project, city as representation, don't mention malls, fast money on the median and the beard nods a sign saying don't look at me. Pick up the union card and the jack thumbs you. Want to read a book, buy a council. Put it on the ballot, build a stadium instead. Sky box replaces how-to.

Meanwhile I'm busted; did a week's in two days, cooked the crackers for the speaker, left for the desert. Packed and taxes after the 5:00 rush. You got sunscreen? Who's in the way back? Bill's in arrears; Jennifer says she'll appeal. No one's got time for the body at taxes. They'll kill 24 hours on the ga-ga scope, make up a sitcom out of incest. I feel constructed, part television part index finger. Then we go up to the airport, say some blather, drink icewater. They make noise and we get the check, engines running on the tarmack. Watch the monitor for your delay function, they sell out and buy up a new bank. You stay at the sleepy traveller, towellette and rubber hat included. When they lived under Socialism there was someone to talk to, now they work alone and take the drugs they used to dispense. Believe me, it's on the news.

The Canal

I'd be gone with the dark sounds
gurgling in the canal,
the ones they let glide past the bridges
and the vowels that no one misses
since almost wind, and of course
I would achieve perfect solitude
me and the music
by men who have lost their hearing
in order to write the late quartets;
I'd be submerged, the speakers
tickling every orifice as I swim past
rocks clicking
in an undulent billiard,
or those grey hulks
out of Shakespeare looming up
against the dock
or could be the heart
in a vault of which this silent typing
is a scant record,
but one persists, turns up the volume
and thinks of the neighbors,
their nakedness a matter of conjecture
as I train the lens on you, auditor
auditorium, atheneum,
"that's what I call a magnifier," he says,
as I rise from the depths
for the first time, unspeakable,
and start over.

Other O Books

Towards The Primeval Lightning Field, Will Alexander. $10.50
Return of the World, Todd Baron, $8.50
A Certain Slant of Sunlight, Ted Berrigan, $9.00
Talking in Tranquility: Interviews with Ted Berrigan, Ted Berrigan, Avenue B and
    O Books, $10.50 (Out of Print)
Mob, Abigail Child, $9.50
Moira, Norma Cole, $9.00
It Then, Danielle Collobert, $9.00
Lapses, John Crouse, $8.00
Candor, Alan Davies, $9.00
Rome, Jerry Estrin, Roof Books and Potes & Poets with O Books, $9.00
Turn Left in Order to Go Right, Norman Fischer, $9.00
Precisely the Point Being Made, Norman Fischer, Chax Press and O Books, $10.00
Time Rations, Benjamin Friedlander, $8.50
byt, William Fuller, $8.50
The Sugar Borders, William Fuller, $9.00
Phantom Anthems, Robert Grenier, $9.00
What I Believe Transpiration/Transpiring Minnesota, Robert Grenier, $24.00
Fray, Jessica Grim, $10.00
The Inveterate Life, Jessica Grim, $8.50
Memory Play, Carla Harryman, $8.50
The Quietist, Fanny Howe, $8.00
VEL, P. Inman, $9.00
The History of the Loma People, Paul D. Korvah, $9.00
Curve, Andrew Levy, $10.00
Values Chauffeur You, Andrew Levy, $9.00
Dreaming Close By, Rick London, $7.00
Abjections, Rick London, $3.50
Dissuasion Crowds the Slow Worker, Lori Lubeski, $8.50
The Case, Laura Moriarty, $11.50
Criteria, Sianne Ngai, $10.00
Close to me & Closer ... (The Language of Heaven) and Désamère, Alice Notley,
    $10.50
Catenary Odes, Ted Pearson, $7.00
Collision Center, Randall Potts, $9.00
(where late the sweet) BIRDS SANG, Stephen Ratcliffe, $8.00
Visible Shivers, Tom Raworth, $8.00
Kismet, Pat Reed, $8.00
Cold Heaven, Camille Roy, $9.00

The Seven Voices, Lisa Samuels, $10.00

O ONE/AN ANTHOLOGY ed. Leslie Scalapino, $10.50

O TWO/AN ANTHOLOGY: *What is the inside, what is outside?,* $10.50

0/4: Subliminal Time, $10.50

Crowd and not evening or light, Leslie Scalapino,$9.00

The India Book: Essays and Translations, Andrew Schelling, $9.00

A's Dream, Aaron Shurin, $8.00

In Memory of My Theories, Rod Smith, $10.50

Homing Devices, Liz Waldner, $9.00.

Picture of The Picture of The Image in The Glass, Craig Watson, $8.00